Princess Diana

THE BOOK
OF LOVE

Princess Diana

THE BOOK OF LOVE

*Words of comfort, joy, and wisdom
from our Queen of Hearts*

Eagle Rose Publishing

Princess Diana

THE BOOK OF LOVE

First published in paperback in 1997 by
Frenbray Pty. Limited, Sydney, Australia

Published in North America and the United Kingdom
by Eagle Rose Publishing. Distributed in North America
and the United Kingdom by Celestial Arts, P.O. Box
7123, Berkeley, CA 94707. (800) 841-2665

Editor: Brian Blackwell

Cover and Book Design: Paula Morrison

Printed in Canada

This little book remembers Diana,
Princess of Wales, our own Queen of Hearts.
It contains the words she spoke about her life,
her loves, her sons, and her beliefs.

It is a reminder of the wonderful woman
she was. Her words, ringing with honesty,
will live on forever.

We hope you will enjoy reading Diana's
words of comfort, joy, love, and wisdom for
many years to come.

She seemed a thing that could not feel
The touch of earthly years.

—*William Wordsworth, 1770–1850*

Life is just a journey.

Diana speaking to friends, 1990

I want my boys to have an understanding of people's emotions, their insecurities, people's distress, and their hopes and dreams.

Diana in the Panorama TV interview, 1995

She made her sighs to sing.
And all things with so sweet a sadness move.
As made my heart at once both grieve and love.

—Anonymous, 16th century

The kindness and affection from the public have carried me through some of the most difficult periods, and always your love and affection have eased the journey.

Diana talking to a group of women, 1993

Anywhere I see suffering,
that is where I want to be,
doing what I can.

Diana talking to friends, 1995

I live for my sons . . .
I would be lost without them.

Diana speaking to friends, 1994

O Diana fair, beyond compare!
I'll make a garland o' thy hair!
Shall bind my heart for evermair,
Until the day I die.

—*Anonymous*

I am all about caring.
I have always been like that.

Diana speaking to a gathering of charity workers
in London

I travelled among unknown men
    In lands beyond the sea;
Nor, England! did I know till then
    What love I bore to thee.
Among thy mountains did I feel
    The joy of my desire;
And she I cherished turned her wheel
    Beside an English fire.

      —William Wordsworth, 1770–1850

I don't want expensive gifts;
I don't want to be bought.
I have everything I want.
I just want someone to be there for
me, to make me feel safe and secure.

Diana speaking to a close friend, 1997

The greatest problem in the world today is intolerance. Everyone is so intolerant of each other.

Diana on a visit to Angola, January 1997

Oh, Rosa, I do so love my boys.

*Diana talking to Rosa Monckton, after a visit to a
Greek church just a few days before she died*

Dear loss! since thy untimely fate
My task hath been to meditate
On thee, on thee: thou are the book,
The library whereon I look.

—*Henry King, 1592–1669*

If I am to care for people in hospital I really must know every aspect of their treatment and understand their suffering.

Diana talking to a close friend about why she watched open heart surgery operations, 1994

I understand people's suffering, people's pain, more than you will ever know yourself.

Diana speaking to a church bishop, 1989

I want to walk into a room, be it a
hospice for the dying or a hospital
for sick children, and feel that I am
needed. I want to do,
not just to be.

Diana talking to friends, 1993

Gather ye rosebuds while ye may,
Old Time is still a-flying:
And this same flower that smiles today,
Tomorrow will be dying.

—*Robert Herrick, 1591–1674*

Whatever happens to me in this relationship (with Dodi), I will continue to do my work, and to help where I am needed.

Diana talking to friend Rosa Monckton,
shortly before her death

I like to be a free spirit. Some don't like that, but that's the way I am.

Diana speaking to friends, 1995

When Spring, with dewy fingers cold,
Returns to deck their hallowed mould,
She there shall dress a sweeter sod
Than Fancy's feet have ever trod.

—*William Collins, 1721–1759*

Whoever is in distress can call me.
I will come running wherever they
are.

Diana quoted by charity workers, 1996

Dodi is a fantastic man.
He covers me with attention and
with care. I feel newly loved.

Diana talking to Cindy Crawford,
a few weeks before her death

When you are happy,
you can forgive a great deal.

Diana talking to close friend Lady Elsa Bowker,
shortly before her death

Beauty, truth, and rarity,
Grace in all simplicity,
Here enclosed in cinders lie.

—*William Shakespeare, 1564–1616*

I'm aware that people
I have loved who have died
are in the spirit world
and look after me.

Diana talking to friends, 1980

Weep you no more, sad fountains;
What need you flow so fast?
Look how the snowy mountains
Heaven's sun doth gently waste.
But my sun's heavenly eyes
View not your weeping,
That now lies sleeping
Softly, now softly lies
 Sleeping.
Sleep is a reconciling,
A rest that peace begets.
Doth not the sun rise smiling
When fair at even he sets?
Rest you then, rest, sad eyes,
Melt not in weeping,
While she lies sleeping
Softly, now softly lies
 Sleeping.

    —Anonymous, 16th century

I've got to have a place
where I can find peace of mind.

Diana talking to friends, 1996

Helping people in need is a good and essential part of my life, a kind of destiny.

Diana speaking to friends, 1993

This boy is dead now. I knew it
before taking him in my arms.
I can remember his face, his
suffering, his voice.

This photo is very dear to me.

Diana talking to friends about a photo taken in
Pakistan, February 1996

How sleep the brave, who sink to rest
By all their country's wishes blest!

—*Anonymous, 17th century*

I am thinking of you constantly.
You are in my prayers throughout
the day. Keep strong, Ivy.
You're a very special lady and
much adored by me.

Diana in a note to Ivy Woodward,
who was recovering from a stroke

But at my back I always hear
Time's winged chariot hurrying near.
And yonder all before us lie
Deserts of vast eternity.

—*Andrew Marvell, 1621–1678*

Every one of us needs to show
how much we care for each other
and, in the process, care for
ourselves.

Diana quoted by friends, 1993

All my past life is mine no more;
  The flying hours are gone,
Like transitory dreams given o'er
Whose images are kept in store
  By memory alone.

—John Wilmot, Earl of Rochester,
1647–1680

I adore him . . .
I have never been so happy.
I have real love.

Diana talking to Lady Elsa Bowker,
shortly before her death

I am always going to be true to myself.

Diana speaking to friends, 1995

True friendships are hugely valuable. We've stuck together through hell and back.

Note to Rosa Monckton, 1997

I'd like to be the queen
of people's hearts.

Diana in the Panorama TV interview, 1995

I've always thought that people need to feel good about themselves and I see my role as offering support to them, to provide some light along the way.

Diana talking to close friends, 1995

Is it a weakness that I lead from my heart, and not my head?

Diana talking to friends, 1995

A heart as soft, a heart as kind,
A heart as sound and free,
As in the whole world thou canst find,
That heart I'll give to thee.

—*Robert Herrick, 1591–1674*

Family is the most important thing
in the world.

Diana speaking to a group of women, 1993

Death doesn't frighten me.

Diana talking to friends, 1994

Carry out a random act
of kindness, with no expectation
of reward, safe in the knowledge
that one day someone might do
the same for you.

Diana quoted by friends, 1993

You can't comfort the afflicted
without afflicting the comfortable.

*A note on Diana's desk
in Kensington Palace*

The people who I care about are the people out there on the street. I can identify with them.

Diana talking to friends, 1996

We have short time to stay, as you,
We have as short a Spring;
As quick a growth to meet decay,
As you or any thing.
We die, as your hours do, and dry away,
Like to the Summer's rain;
Or as the pearls of morning's dew,
Ne'er to be found again.

—Robert Herrick, 1591–1674

I love to hold people's hands when I visit hospitals, even though they are sometimes shocked because they haven't experienced anything like it before. But to me it is a normal thing to do.

Diana talking to friends, 1994

Don't call me an icon.
I'm just a mother trying to help.

Diana speaking to charity workers, 1994

I wear my heart on my sleeve.

Diana talking to charity workers, 1989

Everyone needs to be valued.
Everyone has the potential
to give something back.

Diana speaking to charity workers, 1995

Must I then see, alas eternal night
Sitting upon those fairest eyes,
And closing all those beams
Which once did rise
So radiant and bright.

*—Edward Herbert, Baron Herbert
of Cherbury, 1583–1648*

I have a woman's instinct
and it's always a good one.

Diana talking to friends, 1992

I love Dodi's gentleness and kindness. I like the way he sends flowers and conducts himself.

Diana talking to friends, 1997

If you find someone you love
in your life, then hang on to that
love.

Diana talking to friends, 1995

I love meeting people
and helping them.

Diana talking to friends, 1996

I'd like people to think of me as someone who cares about them.

Diana speaking to charity workers, 1996

I knew what my job was;
it was to go out and meet
the people and love them.

Diana talking to friends, 1995

Anything to make people happy.

Diana speaking about her hospital visits
with the dying

Call me Diana, not Princess Diana.

Diana to hospital patients and on
charity visits, on many occasions

It's vital the monarchy
keeps in touch with the people.
It's what I try to do.

Diana speaking to charity workers, 1994

So many people supported me through my public life and I will never forget them.

Diana talking to friends, 1996

I know that I can give love for a minute, for half an hour, for a day, for a month, but I can give and I'm very happy to do that and I want to do that.

Diana in the Panorama TV interview, 1995

I think the biggest disease this world suffers from in this day and age is the disease of people feeling unloved.

Diana in the Panorama TV interview, 1995

I wish all the mothers, fathers, and children out there realise how much I need them and how I value their love and support.

Diana speaking to charity workers, 1995

My first thoughts
are that I should not
let people down,
that I should support
them and love them.

Diana talking to friends, 1995

How small a part of time they share;
That are so wondrous sweet and fair.

—*Edmund Waller, 1606–1687*

I will fight for my children on any level so they can reach their potential as human beings and in their public duties.

Diana talking to friends, 1995

Bid me to weep, and I will weep,
While I have eyes to see;
And having none, yet I will keep
A heart to weep for thee.

—*Robert Herrick, 1591–1674*

She kept company with kings and queens, with princes and presidents, but we especially remember ... how she met individuals and made them feel significant. In her death she commands the sympathy of millions.

—*Dr. Wesley Carr, Dean of Westminster,*
at Diana's funeral

If I should die
and leave you here awhile,
be not like others,
sore undone, who keep
long vigils by
the silent dust, and weep.
For my sake—turn
to life again and smile,

nerving thy heart
and trembling hand to do
something to comfort
other hearts than thine.
Complete those dear
unfinished tasks of mine
and I, perchance
may therein comfort you.

—Poem read by Lady Sarah
McCorquodale, Diana's eldest sister,
at the funeral

I vow to thee, my country,
all earthly things above,
entire and whole and perfect,
the service of my love;
the love that asks no question,
the love that stands the test,

that lays upon the altar
the dearest and the best;
the love that never falters,
the love that pays the price,
the love that makes undaunted
the final sacrifice.

And there's another country,
I've heard of long ago,
most dear to them that love her,
most great to them that know;
we may not count her armies,
we may not see her King;

her fortress is a faithful heart,
her pride is suffering;
and soul by soul and silently
her shining bounds increase,
and her ways are ways of gentleness
and all her paths are peace.

—A hymn by Cecil Spring-Rice
sung at Diana's funeral

Time is too slow for those who wait,
too swift for those who fear,
too long for those who grieve,
too short for those who rejoice,
but for those who love,
time is eternity.

—Poem read by Lady Jane Fellowes,
Diana's elder sister, at the funeral

… And now abideth
faith,
   hope,
     love,
       these three;
but the greatest of these
       is love.

    —*1 Corinthians 13, read by Prime
    Minister Tony Blair at the funeral*

Lord, we thank you for Diana whose life touched us all and for all those memories of her that we treasure.

—*Dr. George Carey, Archbishop of Canterbury, at the funeral*

She was the people's princess and that is how she will stay, how she will remain in our hearts and our memories forever.

—Tony Blair

Princess Diana had become an ambassador for victims of land mines, war orphans, the sick and needy throughout the world.

—Nelson Mandela

Hillary and I knew her, and I'm so glad
I met her. We are deeply saddened by this
tragic event.

— *Bill Clinton*

All she ever thought about was other
people.

— *Richard Branson*

The world has lost the most
compassionate of humanitarians,
and someone so special.

— *Sarah, Duchess of York*

With her tragic death a beacon of light
has been extinguished.

—*Margaret Thatcher*

She was irreplaceable.

—*Luciano Pavarotti*

She's gone now but it's up to us to carry
on her work and help people who need it.

—*Elton John*

With her death, all joy vanished, all pleasures, entertainments, and delights were overcast and darkness covered the face of the Court. She was its light and life. She was everywhere at once, she was its centre; her presence permeated its inner life.... No princess was ever so sincerely mourned, none was ever more worth regretting.

—*Anonymous, 18th century*

FAREWELL

Hail to thee, blithe Spirit!

—*Percy Bysshe Shelley, 1792–1822*

FAREWELL

Her mirth the world required
She bath'd it in smiles of glee.
But her heart was tired, tired
And now they let her be.
Her life was turning, turning
In mazes of heat and sound,
For peace her soul was yearning
And now peace laps her round.
Her cabin'd ample spirit,
It fluttered and failed for breath.
Tonight it doth inherit
the vasty halls of death.

—*Matthew Arnold, 1822–1888*